Inspiration on Demand

Joshua Coburn

Inspiration on Demand

Copyright 2013
Joshua Coburn

All internal photography, artwork, layout, and design
by Carmen DeJong

Backcover photo by Drew Ruggles

All right reserved under International and Pan-American Copyright Conventions.

Published in the United States by Provoke Productions.
No selections from this book, whole or in part, may be used without the written permission of the publisher.
Printed by Signature Book Printing
www.sbpbooks.com

ISBN:978-0-9754304-2-2

Joshua Coburn
For Speaking, Coaching, & Mentoring
Contact 641-990-5019

Iowa
www.facebook.com/joshua.coburn13
#ihelpedchangealife

Special Thanks
To My Beautiful Wife
& Amazing Children

A Note from the Author

I originally thought I had this project ready to roll. Editing was done, covers were being readied, and the funding & marketing plans laid out, what more was there to do? Then, thousands of feet above the western United States on an airplane headed toward the sprawling metropolis that is Los Angeles, I realized I had done something wrong, drastically wrong. I had, personally, treated this book as a project rather than something personal.

Inspiration on Demand is not a project; it is an honest look at the daily struggles of an individual who, at times, was filled with strength and courage, other times torn with insecurities, and yet other moments full of questions about where life would lead. At this moment, I am headed to a place I had dreamed of going since I was a child. To be honest, I am scared that to be entering a city of 18 million alone but at the same time I am also excited for the unknown, deeply saddened to leave my family behind for days at a time, and also determined to achieve what I have come to this city to do.

I am human; these emotions, all emotions I experience, are not uncommon for all of us to wrestle with in our lives. It is this link between us all that makes me realize I was mistaken in treating Inspiration on Demand as a project. In fact, emotion is the very reason why Inspiration on Demand exists. The conception of positive affirmations and messages allowed me to remain creative during what

I would have likely referred to as a creative "dead period" for me in my life. I say so because I had mostly stopped all effort on internalized creative works, or so I thought. I was searching for a way to start each morning off with a tone that would allow me to have positive and forward momentum in place, mentally, as I moved through each day's obstacles. My posting of these positive affirmations and messages was purely to keep me honest. I thought that if others read what I had to say, I had darn well be living it when people saw me face to face.

 Truth be known, it did. Little by little I started to see my attitudes change. The smiles on the faces of individuals I met each day fueled me to keep posting, and acting upon, these messages. Ultimately others started to catch on, passing me words of encouragement and letting me know how they had planned to pay it forward, to remain optimistic, and to share this incredible positivity with one another.

 If there is anything I can say about me, personally, let me say this, I am not perfect, far from it, and I am proud of that. I failed to consider the emotional investment, not only that I had made in this book, but also the emotional investment you all had made as well. For that I apologize, though I am proud that my mistakes, fears, insecurities, triumphs, daily smiles, thoughts of unity, and ultimately, fight for the realization of dreams & optimism has been identified with and I am honored to be able to openly share my life with all of you. Most importantly, I am honored that anyone took a moment out of their busy life to let me know that my daily messages resonated with them in one way or another.

Here's to the moments when we inspire and are inspired by others, to the moments when we are afraid to be vulnerable but risk the chance of pain anyway, here's to the moments when we can acknowledge that we are all flawed and accept that this is what makes us all individually great yet similar at the same time. I am afraid, I am flawed, but you have all proven that is ok, that being vulnerable is worth the risk, that the rewards are immense and wonderful. Here's to working together to overcome all odds and obstacles. Here's to the creation of Inspiration on Demand, to the dedication everyone involved had in making this book a reality, and to the positive moments when we can all join together to create and inspire one another. It is to those moments that I dedicate this book, and to all of you for being a part of it.

Thank you.
 –Joshua Coburn

Inspiration on Demand

Inspiration on Demand was created out of a project called I Helped Change a Life— a mission based on personal necessity, founded by accident and created by a community.

Like many of us who struggle to stay positive, I had been—for years—posting positive affirmations for myself each morning on various social media platforms. Thousands of social media users began to comment, "Like", and suggest that they wanted to see a compilation of these affirmations for daily reference and to share with others who were also struggling.

Because so many people suggested that I do a book, I realized that the project was as much about their wants as it was for my own need for positive reinforcement. The answer to those wants and needs became I Helped Change a Life. This project allowed social media users to help create the book everyone said I should write. They chose the title Inspiration on Demand. They also chose the dimensions, cover style, and all other aspects. In return, they received free signed print copies, signed & personalized posters, and an opportunity to be included as a contributor to the work. Not only did they collaboratively create this book, they changed my life, their own lives and the lives of others with whom they chose to share this book.

Together we created Inspiration on Demand. Hopefully, it will positively impact the lives of all who read it. No matter the results, making this book has inspired me and provided me a new family full of friends. It's given me an overwhelming of sense of pride, and caused me to intensely and personally reflect. I Helped Change a Life is not about me. It's about the process of working together to create and deliver a positive message to the world.

I would like to personally thank each and every contributor and participant who pushed me to create a project that would allow me to learn to let go while developing a book, a project, and a community more amazing than I could have dreamed.

If you wish to view the full creation of Inspiration on Demand please follow Joshua Coburn's Facebook profile at www.facebook.com/joshuacoburn13 or in pictures on Instagram at #ihelpedchangealife.

Smile, it changes your life,
and your world.

Starting over should be seen as a
chance at new opportunities which
can be viewed as future success.

The hard lessons that come of seeing your flaws allow you to focus on fixing them.

Listen when others are speaking, don't just hear their words.
The information provided can change your life.

Dreams have no time limits or expiration dates. Dreams do not have to be executed perfectly either. If you are living with a smile on your face, you are already successful. Keep moving forward happily with a goal in mind; chances are good you will eventually reach it.

No matter the amount of pain caused,
forgiving those who caused it results in peace.

Knowing your personal limits
is as important as pushing them.

• • ●

Often a single word can embody all that we are, today that word is Courage! Have the courage to step out of your comfort zone, courage to face your fears, courage to take a risk, & courage to evolve into who you believe you can be, beyond what you already are.

● • •

The hounds may be nipping at our heels regularly, rather than run it is best to stop and fight them off once and for all.

If you're working toward a dream and need inspiration, turn around and look how far you've already come. There is inspiration in your own hard work. The satisfaction of fulfilling a dream is only eclipsed by the realization of how hard you've worked to get there and the feeling of success it brings.

Happiness takes a lot of
work, but all the best things
in life are earned. Work
hard to achieve this frame of
mind today & every day!

•

•

●

When climbing the ladder of happiness, look to the top to reach your goal, but focus only on the next rung and take each step with a smile.

• • ●

The moments just before dawn, when the low light silhouettes the distant landscape, remind yourself, anywhere on this Earth is a place of solitude because we can see this same sight from any location in the world. How peaceful.

● ● •

Anger is an emotional prison,
the keys to unlock the doors lie
in the pursuit of happiness.

Even in darkness
we must search for the light.
Without hope we have
nothing!

• • ●

Accidents happen, but when you fall off the wagon—get up, climb back on, and get moving. No use wasting time wallowing in your mistakes

● ● •

Having a dream is the first
step to achieving one!

If the drive to succeed is fueled by smiles, the road ahead will be paved with happiness.

Measure your success only by the positive ways in which you affect the lives of other's, the contagious smiles which you spread, and the emotional bonds which you build.

●

Only an open heart can be wounded
and we all must remember that the
risk is worth its weight in love.

●

Illumination of the positive sends a light to all those around us. Today, illuminate your being and get contagious.

●

Today make the choice to be happy
and to utilize your strength, integrity,
and hope, in order to have the proper
supplies you need to begin a new path
on life's journey.

A handshake is the first step to achieving a hug!

To live a life of righteousness we must not only be the best person we can be when it comes easy, we must fight to be the best person we can be when it doesn't.

●

●

●

Our lives are not defined by the goals we reach, but instead by the integrity which we uphold while striving to reach them.

We are successful because we smile and overcome negative thoughts.

Cup your hands together
& peer inside. They appear
empty but know they are
overflowing with the power
to achieve your dreams.

●

●

●

Let go of yesterday, as well as the fear of
tomorrow, in order to focus more clearly on the
privileges of waking on this beautiful morning
when so many were unable to do so.

Say aloud "I am confident;
I will overcome any challenge today,
regardless of size!"

• • ●

Today, make others smile.

● • •

Primal therapy is pure and good!
Step outside and let out a scream this morning!

The only road to happiness
is the road you pave yourself.

•

•

•

> The obstacles on today's journey are
> the foundation for tomorrow's stories of
> inspiration & overcoming adversity.

We dictate who we are and how we act.
No one can take this from us.

• • ●

We are not only strong, but beautiful and today we will prove it.

● • •

Make your personal sun shine every day, regardless of the weather.

*Life is like any other structure,
it needs a solid foundation
and frame or it will crumble.*

If there is darkness it is only because
we need to see that the light is shining
brighter at the end of the tunnel.

●

●

●

***If there is not a path to follow
we shall create our own.***

Remain positive in the face of adversity
in order to reassure yourself, and others,
of our personal strengths.

• • ●

> Refuse to let others
> control your emotions.

● • •

Realizing that both sides of
the bed are the same prevents
any chance of waking on the
wrong side of it.

Remind yourself to calmly accept your insecurities and firmly push them aside because you have many important qualities to offer the world.

•

•

•

Today step one foot after another, keep moving forward in order to create a positive impact on the lives of anyone encountered!

A dream is only a goal which we haven't reached yet.

Each of us has baggage that we tend to haul around with us regularly. Lighten the load today, open it up, empty the contents, and stop wasting valuable energy.

Believe you can do anything;
you may be surprised by the results!

• • ●

You cannot see the fruits
of your labor unless you've
planted the seeds.

● • •

When we arrive at a fork in the road,
a choice of the left or right hand
path, forge straight ahead & create
one of your own.

The amount of responsibility which we currently bear must be viewed in a positive light.
We only take on as much as we can handle.

Study the face of those most important to you as often as possible. Sadly, none of us last forever and the memories will be cherished.

When climbing life's mountains, remember that there will be slips, stumbles, and falls but each step takes us closer to the peak and the view from the top is only as rewarding as the journey.

Remind yourself of how blessed you are with people that care about you as well as those we are able to care for. Nothing in life could be more important.

• • •

Our struggles are simply lessons in disguise!

• • •

Though our dreams may seem far in the distance, the steps to get there are always within walking distance.

Choose to change every occurrence of the word FEAR in your life to ADVENTURE!

Each day is like the sprinkles
on a doughnut, full of variety
and always really good!

Barter for the things most important to you.
Start with a hug, you'll surely get one back!

Remember the little things,
stop & smell the roses,
pass along a friendly smile,
and to tell those you care about
that you love them.

Say "Hello" to everyone you see today,
stranger or otherwise.
You'll marvel at the lives you change.

• • ●

A place of happiness is a place with family,
blood or otherwise.

● • •

Smile like you mean it,
none of us have much time left.
Appreciate every second.

Today is the best tomorrow that yesterday could have ever offered.

•

•

•

In the desert of life, water is only found when you are continuously searching for it.

We cannot be upset by the cold,
seeing our breath reminds us we are alive.

If a smile can make someone's day,
imagine what a hug can do.

Though dark clouds hover menacingly above, focus on the majesty of each droplet of precipitation as well as nature's unblemished fragrance from the fresh rainfall.

If you see someone, even a stranger, struggling to smile today, give them a reason.

It's unbelievable the impact people from your past can have on your future.

• • ●

It is an honor to be a part of today; many did not make it through the night. We must never forget that.

● • •

It's amazing where a road can take you if you let someone else be your guide once in a while.

Happiness is always within reach. It's just a matter of outstretching your arm and grabbing hold!

Today carry yourself with poise, strength, & confidence while remaining humble & open to positive growth.

Today stop taking the road less traveled; it is still a road that has been traveled and leads to someone else's destination. Begin pulling weeds on your own path, choosing your own destiny.

If you want to be successful in
moving mountains you must
start by moving that first stone.

• • ●

Success can be measured by any set
of criteria, but it is your perspective
that allows you to reach it.

● • •

The bottom rung is just the first step
on the ascent to greatness!

Having strength & courage doesn't mean you're fearless, it means you do what you have to do regardless of fear.

●

●

●

Listen, love, and support everyone around you, you may be all they've got.

Our places in the world aren't obvious, it takes a lot of hard lessons, time, and work, but if you never get started you'll never get there.

Never forget to say "I love you" to those close to you, the opportunity doesn't last forever.

Reach for the sky,
especially when you are the farthest from it.

Wake, appreciate that you can enjoy another day, focus on happiness, commit to making at least one stranger smile, be passionate about being alive, and take at least one healthy stride toward a dream.

Dismantling emotional road blocks comes with high risks, but yields results beyond imagination.

• • ●

The unexpected twists & turns in life are often the most rewarding challenges we will ever face.

● ● •

Confidence is never compromising your integrity for others and happily living by your own standards.

While it's important to mold your life to reach your destination, sometimes we must remember to relax and let life mold us.

•
•
•

Knowledge is the wonderful thing
that one cannot get enough of
nor can retain to the point of using
all which has been sought.

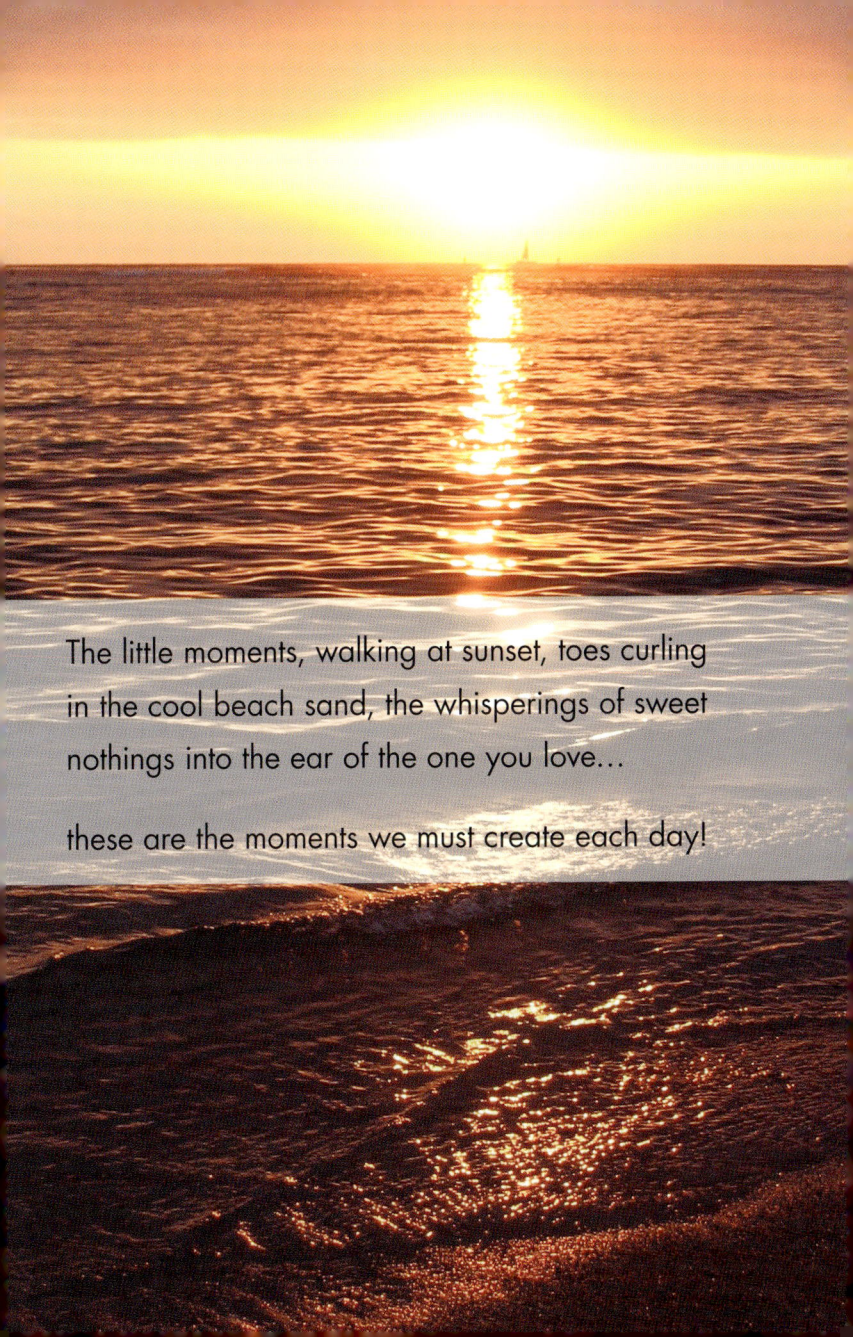

The little moments, walking at sunset, toes curling in the cool beach sand, the whisperings of sweet nothings into the ear of the one you love...

these are the moments we must create each day!

Love starts as friendship;
friendship starts with one word,
"Hello".

• • ●

Changing your life is simple when
you stop talking about it and start doing it.

● • •

Reaching your goals is a matter
of finding where your heart is and
then making your feet get there.

Determination is what fills the gap between the excitement of beginning a journey and the satisfaction of completing it.

Integrity is not gained from words you speak, but instead by the actions you take.

Fill each day with moment's
worth remembering.

• • ●

Deviate from the norm, it is the
only way for extraordinary people
to do extraordinary things.

● • •

A positive day always begins
with a positive thought.

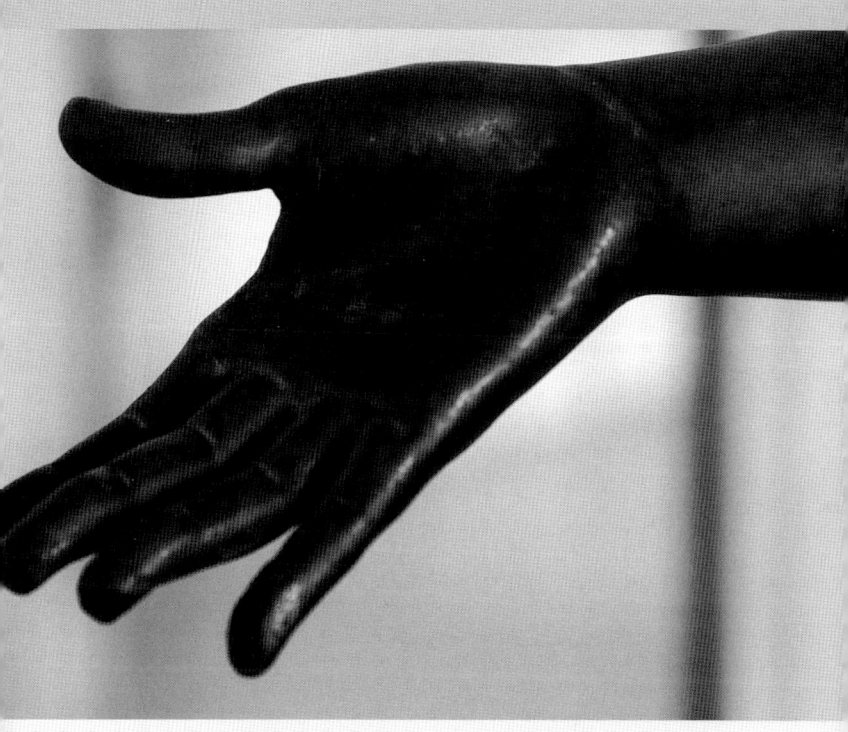

Open your arms, extend a hand,
or say "Good Morning",
you may change the course
of someone's day, possibly life,
and they may change yours.

With patience & persistence
we can weather any storm.

• • ●

By day's end, be sure you can look back
and know you made the best of it.

● • •

Time is the most precious gift,
and give it as often as you can
to everyone you meet.

In order to make a change in life, we must first make a commitment to actually making that change.

Don't believe you can make your dreams
come true, know you can.

• • ●

Don't be upset you have to get up early,
be happy you get to see the sun rise!

● • •

Approach today with force and might,
ready to overcome all obstacles
in a positive manner!

Calmly place anger safely under lock & key to allow the presence of only happiness.

Pressure is just a reminder that you are great and people have expectations that keep you on track to reach even higher levels of greatness.

●

●

●

A hero is not someone who does something great, a hero is someone who is honest about what he does and gives credit where it's due.

●

Find joy in the fulfillment of others
and you, yourself, will be fulfilled.

●

An enemy is just a friend
you have yet to forgive.

●

Another beautiful day,
a reminder of how privileged
we are to be alive.

Average can be avoided by being exceptional.

• • ●

Don't just believe you can
make your dreams come true,
know you can.

● • •

Share a smile,
they're infectious!

When standing at the bottom of a mountain looking at the thousands of feet between yourself and the summit, remember that reaching the peak is as simple as choosing to put one foot in front of the other.

Communicate. People all around you are hurting, needing a hand, and still wearing a mask of happiness because they don't want to "burden you". The cracks show quickly when you show you care. Be kind, ask questions, smile, give a hug, and don't forget, someday you'll be hurting too and need that smile, that hug, and that motivation. Give some of yourself, live for others; it will change your life!

Remember, it is about the little things.
Enjoy them often.

Today there is no lack of things to do, no lack of risks to take, no lack of inspiration to be found, and no lack of reason to smile. Plan to push limits, to reach out to people, and do your best to give a positive influence to others.

Negativity only enters your life if you allow it, refuse.

• • ●

Failure doesn't exist, only lessons
on the way to success.

● • •

Accepting past hurt gives way to
future patience, grace, & wisdom.

Take the reins of life's wild horses,
pull them together,
& give them direction!

Inspiration is everything and it is all around us, the stranger next to you, the world around you, see it in all things.

No matter the amount of pain caused, forgiving those who caused it results in peace.

If life is what you make it,
make each day positive for
ourselves, and one another,
in order to make all lives
positively fulfilling.

• • ●

Motivation starts with addressing your shortcomings and ends with overcoming them.

● • •

Showing the world

who you are and

make a stand for it

all the same.

Life is good, take some time to soak in the moments that matter, we are not here long.

• • ●

Remind yourself that you matter, that making mistakes is a learning experience, and life is about treating people well. Don't forget to smile every chance you get.

Your scars are who you are; the lines on your face are your lessons, and your positive attitude about them is your representation to the world a willingness to share all you've gained.

Gaining respect takes work,
but upholding it takes a lifetime.

While on new paths, fear is
erased by joining hands and
traveling together.

Changing your perspective is all it takes
to change your view of life!

•
•
•

Inspire others by your actions, live well, be honest & truthful, and support others. My hand is waiting to assist in getting others on their feet, not because they need help, but because it is better than going it alone. We can all use a hand once in a while; get yours out there for others too.

Live to inspire others and be open
enough to let others inspire you

• • ●

Refuse to let others bring you down to
your knees, instead be determined to help
them rise to their feet!

● • •

Know that you have the
power to choose what each
day in your life will be like!

Today is a great day to be alive!
Often we forget how little we are in such a big world,
be happy to be in it!

There are many amazing people out there, be one of them.

• • ●

Fight hard to overcome your obstacles.
Rise up to any occasion.
Be true to yourself and others.

● ● •

Determination is the difference between getting through & giving up and success is the driven state of mind you have while on that journey.

A cold, silent morning before the dawn really reminds me of how peaceful this world can be. Before the muffled voices, driving cars, and rustling of paperwork begins there is only silence, the sky, and my breath visually manifesting in front of me. A few minutes to take it all in sets a wondrous memory in my mind.

.
.
●

Each of us occasionally hit a wall but we must not forget that it can be dismantled one brick at a time.

Look North!
It is the only positive direction!

Success is always behind a smile!

Look for the best in everyone
and focus on the positive!

Words, the most powerful weapon we have.
Use them wisely and wield them with wisdom.

• • ●

> Living is not about controlling
> what occurs in your life, but about
> controlling how you react to what
> occurs in your life.

● ● •

If a situation is beyond your control,
the situation is beyond your worry.

The things you want in life, they are there, you are just not there yet. Work hard for that light at the end of the tunnel... it is waiting for you to arrive.

Stop searching for life's treasures, get out there and start creating them.

-
-
-

Stepping outside yourself and staring down your life's mistakes takes guts but it takes real strength to share them with others in hopes they will not make the same mistakes as you.

The best thing about today is that we get to make the choice to be happy!

• • ●

Stop for a moment, breathe deep, and enjoy the beauty that surrounds you.

● • •

It's a good beginning to what will become a great day!

When the world gets heavy, pick it up, rest it upon your back, and carry. We all need hope, and those that carry the world of hope upon their backs are not burdened, but instead motivated. Pick up & move forward, lead by example, live in inspiration.

Stop searching for life's treasures, get out there and start creating them.

Inspiration on Demand would not have been possible without contributions from the kind and gracious people listed below.

V. Wallerich	Michaela Jo Kirby
Stacia Steffensmeier	Aggie Crabtree
Roy Hill	Loriann Tague
Drew Ruggles	Kristina Romberg
Carmen DeJong	Jake and Wendy Dayton
LaRay Keiser	Jack Nouri
Ryan Repp	Joan McCammant Hunt
Brittney Kuntz	Vicki Watts
Sarah Jean Perry	Teri Plants
Travis Solem	The Hawkins Family
Brandy Virchow	Tiya Montano
Don Coburn	Carla R Kriegel
Krista Humphrey	Jana Hernandez Newport
Danny Gould	Donna M. Baustian
Jessica Lacaeyse	Bill Houlihan
Chandra Tanke	Leah Keller
Monica and Ben Rae	J.B. Paulson
Amy Blankenship	Alice Harden
Nickalena Monk	Christy Kriegel